HAL LEONARD GUITAR METHOD

CLASSICAL GUITAR BOOK 2

ISBN 978-1-4950-5192-0

Visit Hal Leonard Online at
www.halleonard.com

To access audio, visit:
www.halleonard.com/mylibrary

Enter Code
3807-0561-1861-4473

World headquarters, contact:
Hal Leonard
7777 West Bluemound Road
Milwaukee, WI 53213
Email: info@halleonard.com

In Europe, contact:
Hal Leonard Europe Limited
Dettingen Way
Bury St Edmunds, Suffolk, IP33 3YB
Email: info@halleonardeurope.com

In Australia, contact:
Hal Leonard Australia Pty. Ltd.
4 Lentara Court
Cheltenham, Victoria, 3192 Australia
Email: info@halleonard.com.au

INTRODUCTION

Before proceeding, please understand that many of the concepts in this volume are presented with the assumption that the topics and techniques presented in Book One of this series have been understood and mastered to an adequate degree. This will provide a necessary foundation for further success. However, to help ensure your progress, some reminders of basic important points and concepts that were introduced in Book One are also included in this volume. Finally, while this method will present many essential technical and musical concepts that a guitarist should strive to master, it is advisable to seek the help of a well-trained, experienced teacher to help guide you through your individual learning situations.

A CLASSICAL GUITARIST'S PATH TO SUCCESS

There are three important elements of improving your playing and musicianship. Each one of these elements will help with the other. Conversely, neglecting any one of these will hold back the others. Working with a knowledgeable instructor and observing accomplished guitarists and musicians perform will help you address these issues. Most importantly, as you practice on your own, keep the following three elements in mind:

1. Work on technique. The efficient use of your body, hands, and fingers to master a wide variety of techniques is needed to produce an attractive tone with clear articulation. Always use logical and efficient fingering.

2. Understand all aspects of the musical score and be able to accurately read the notes and rhythms.

3. Develop stylistic interpretations and add your own creativity into your playing.

CLEAR SOUNDS AND A LEGATO TONE: TWO IMPORTANT CONCEPTS FOR BEAUTIFUL PLAYING

People who choose to learn to play the classical guitar are often drawn to it because of the beautiful sound it makes in the hands of a good player. While there are many qualities that can make your playing beautiful, the two most basic concepts for a classical guitarist to master are *clarity* and *legato*. One might be able to perform the notes and rhythms of a piece accurately; but, if the notes are not clear and played with *legato* when the music requires, a listener will be challenged to find the beauty in the music. If you place these basic concepts at the forefront of your practicing, they will soon become a valuable foundation of your playing, allowing you to achieve further goals!

Clarity

Clear-sounding notes are largely accomplished by using an articulate right-hand technique, maintaining left-hand accuracy, and using consistent finger pressure for the full duration of a given note. A good player should be able to maintain a consistent, clear, full tone throughout a passage of music.

Legato

Playing legato means that the notes sound connected to each other. Notes that are presented in stepwise or scale form across strings require special attention as both hands must work in synchronization.

> **PRACTICE TIP**
>
> Careful listening and slow practicing are the most effective ways to get quick results.

Use the following simple scale exercise as a warmup. Strive for a legato sound and maintain a consistent, full tone. Practice alternating between both *i* and *m*, and *m* and *a*.

Study No. 1 – Scale Exercise in A Natural Minor

TRACK 1 🔊

The following selections by Fernando Sor and Mauro Giuliani are played completely in *first position*, so no shifting is required. When playing in first position, the first finger on your fretting hand will naturally play the 1st fret. If playing a passage where your first finger naturally plays the 2nd fret, you will be playing in second position (and so on). Playing from memory will allow you to carefully listen to the quality of your playing without the distraction of reading the notes. Once again, strive for a clear, articulate tone and legato lines.

> **PRACTICE TIP**
>
> Take care to use logical right-hand fingering. Use *p* for bass notes with stems pointing down. Alternate right-hand fingers when playing scale passages. Incorporate *i*, *m*, and *a* for arpeggios.

ETUDE IN A MINOR

Fernando Sor

TRACK 2

MAESTOSO

Mauro Giuliani

TRACK 3

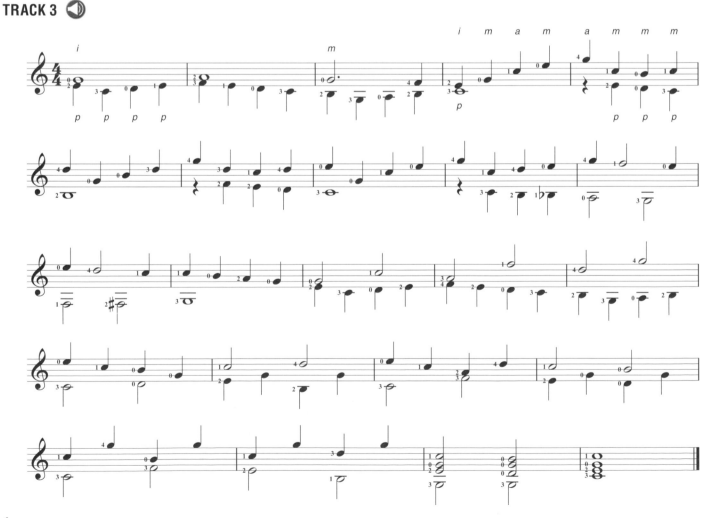

ESTUDIO IN C

Fernando Sor

TRACK 4

FIND THE MELODY AND MAKE IT SING

One thing that is special about the classical guitar style of playing is that it allows you to play melody and accompaniment at the same time. Strive to master the art of playing a beautiful melody while at the same time playing a tasteful accompaniment, each with its own individual sense of phrasing. First make sure you are clear about which notes are part of the melody and which notes are the accompaniment. Because guitar music is written on one staff (unlike piano music), it is a little more difficult to quickly see the separate parts; however, each of the separate voices or parts are usually distinguished by the direction of the stems. The stems on notes containing the melody generally point up, and the stems on the notes containing the accompaniment generally point down.

The best way to approach playing pieces with clearly defined melody and accompaniment parts is to first play each part separately. This will give you a clear concept of what each part should sound like when you later combine the two parts. Finally, you will want to master the skill of playing the melody more prominently than the accompaniment.

ANDANTE IN C

Fernando Sor

TRACK 5 🔊

DYNAMICS

Adding dynamics to the performance of a piece means to vary the volume of the notes being played. Changing the loudness of a note or group of notes can greatly enhance the expressivity of one's playing. While many of these dynamic changes are decided on by the performer's own interpretation, often the composer will indicate these directives on the score.

There are many terms used to indicate dynamics. Below are the most common ones that might be used in a musical selection.

COMMON DYNAMICS SYMBOLS

p or *piano*	Play softly
mp or *mezzo-piano*	Play moderately softly
pp or *pianissimo*	Play very softly
f or *forte*	Play loudly
mf or *mezzo-forte*	Play moderately loudly
ff or *fortissimo*	Play very loudly
crescendo (*cresc.*)	Play gradually louder
diminuendo (*dim.*)	Play gradually softer

Also very common are the symbols for crescendo and diminuendo.

Crescendo   *Diminuendo*

In the following selection by Mauro Giuliani, the melody is in the upper voice (stems up). Work to give that voice more prominence than the accompaniment. This piece also contains dynamic markings which should be followed for an effective performance. Feel free to add more of your own.

ALLEGRETTO

Mauro Giuliani

TRACK 6

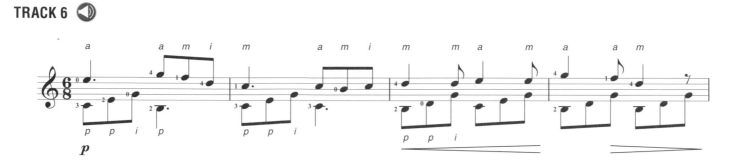

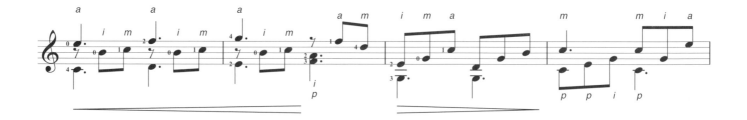

The next piece by Ferdinando Carulli is another example of melody with accompaniment.

ALLEGRETTO

Ferdinando Carulli

2nd time, D.C. al Fine
(no repeats)

DAMPING

Just as it is important to let notes sound for their full duration, it is also necessary to stop or *dampen* the sound of notes so that they do not ring too long and thus conflict with the sound of the notes that follow. Most often, it is the open bass notes that need to be stopped from ringing too long.

Following are a few different short passages in which damping of the bass notes is necessary to eliminate any unwanted over-ringing of the bass notes. In Study No. 2, the low A note needs to be stopped with the right-hand thumb at the half rest on the third beat. This is also the exact time that a finger plays the higher B note. Use the same procedure for the low D, stopping the note from ringing with the thumb while at the same time playing the C above with a finger.

Study No. 2 – Damping Example 1

Dampen A: Use the thumb
to stop the A bass note.

In Study No. 3, the A bass note in measure 1 needs to be stopped when the D bass note is played in measure 2. Using the back of your thumb to quickly stop the A note while also preparing to play the D note is an effective technique. The photo shows the thumb damping the low E at the end of measure 3 while preparing to play the low A in measure 4. The fingers are also creating the rest in measure 4 while preparing to play the final triad.

Study No. 3 – Damping Example 2

Dampen A: Use back of thumb to
stop the A bass note while playing D.

Dampen E: Use back of thumb to
stop the E bass note while playing A.

This technique will also work in the next example when the string to be stopped contains the adjacent lower bass note.

Study No. 4 – Damping Example 3

Bass notes that ring over to clash with a new harmony are the most important ones to stop. Use your ear to decide. There might be times when it is very inconvenient to use your right hand to dampen a particular offending note. In such cases, feel free to try using a free left-hand finger to do the job.

The following piece by Matteo Carcassi will give you an opportunity to try dampening the bass notes as indicated by the rests. **Remember: The rests are telling you to "play" silence.** Following the dynamics and "playing" the rests in this piece will help make it come alive!

ANDANTE

Matteo Carcassi

TRACK 8 🔊

LOW E STRING TUNED TO D

Sometimes a piece requires the low E string to be tuned one whole step lower to D. **This, of course, means that every note on the 6th string will now be located two frets higher than usual.** You may use an electric tuner, but it is a simple task to use your ear to match the sound of the 6th string to the sound of the open D note on the 4th string. The D on the 4th string will sound an octave higher, but it is still easy to hear. You may also double-check the pitch by matching the harmonic on the 12th fret of the 6th string to the exact same pitch of the open 4th string. When tuning before performing a piece, the last step should be to play a chord or two in the key you will be playing, checking for any needed final adjustments.

PRACTICE TIP

Once retuned, the 6th string tends to slightly contract and go a bit sharp. To prevent this, first tune the 6th string a step or two too low before bringing it back up to the D pitch.

Tune your low E string to D to play the following piece by the English Renaissance lute master John Dowland. In the first measure, you might wish to dampen the bass notes with the back of your thumb as you change chords. A sharp ear will help to guide you in keeping the other bass notes under control as you proceed.

ALMAN

John Dowland

TRACK 9

UNDERSTANDING THE FRETBOARD

Once you have mastered locating the notes in first position, learning the notes on the higher frets is the next step. The following diagram shows all the natural notes and their frets on each string. Start by learning to play from memory all the natural notes on the 1st string. Moving from one fret to the next is moving by a half step; moving two frets is a whole step.

The relationships between the notes are the same on each string, and the patterns will repeat again on each string starting at the 12th fret. **So, once you have the pattern of the notes memorized on the 1st string, know the note name of each string, and know how many steps come between each note, you will actually have all the information you need to be able to name every note on every fret of every string!**

Once you are familiar with the natural-note patterns for each string, it is a simple job to fill in the corresponding sharps and flats between each note. Of course, there is not a sharp or flat note between B and C or E and F since they are just a half step apart.

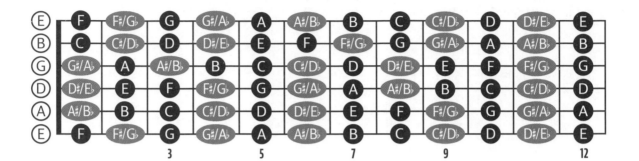

LEFT-HAND SHIFTING

To play the notes in the higher positions, you must shift from the lower frets to the upper frets and back. This should be a simple process if attention is given to a few basic details.

1. Assuming your left thumb is in the proper position while in the lower position, simply use motion from your forearm, rotating from the elbow, to reposition your thumb and fingers on the higher fret group.

2. Allow your thumb and fingers to relax enough to gracefully slide with the movement of your hand so that the thumb position in relationship to the rest of your hand is the same as before the shift. **Do not allow the thumb to drag when shifting.** This is a common issue when first practicing executing a shift, most often when shifting from the lower to higher frets.

3. Take care to resist the urge to reach with your fingers when you shift. It is not the job of the fingers to help with the shift!

4. Follow the same guidelines when shifting back down to the lower frets.

The following simple exercise can be repeated on every string. Saying the name of each note out loud as you play is an excellent way to learn the notes on the fretboard!

Study No. 5 – Chromatic Shifting

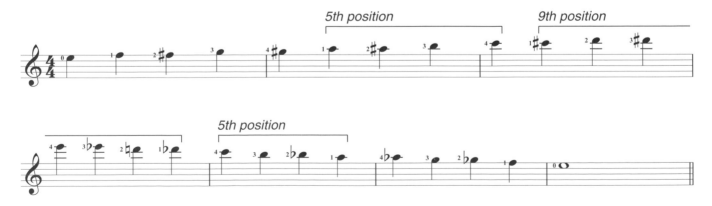

MOVING UP THE FRETS ON THE HIGH E, B, AND G STRINGS

The following study uses notes on the higher frets of the 1st and 2nd strings. Circled numbers near the notes will indicate the string on which to find the note. Included are only a few fingerings at key points in the melody, allowing you to use your note-reading skills to navigate through the piece.

Study No. 6 — Aeolian Melody

TRACK 10

The next composition includes melodies played on higher frets on the 1st and 2nd strings.

MELODY IN E MINOR

Paul Henry

TRACK 11

MOVING UP THE FRETS ON THE D, A, AND LOW E STRINGS

The next three pieces include notes higher up the neck on the bottom three strings.

LECCION IN A MINOR

Fernando Sor

TRACK 12

FERNANDO SOR (1778–1839)

Born in Barcelona in 1778, Fernando Sor attended choir school at the Montserrat Monastery as a young man and later enrolled in Barcelona's military academy. After serving in the military to ward of the French invasion, he relocated to the more intellectually inspiring city of Paris—as many other Spanish artisans did. After two years of performing, composing, and teaching, he moved to London in 1858 where he composed operas, chamber music, and symphonies. Regarded as a major contributor to the classical guitarist's repertoire, he is best known for his wealth of guitar compositions including a popular guitar method, many solo masterpieces, and a large number of exquisite smaller works and etudes.

The arrows in the next piece represent strums. Using the finger shown by the arrow, strum either up or down across the strings. Remember, don't be fooled by the direction of the arrow! The upward-pointing arrow indicates a downstroke, and the downward-pointing arrow indicates an upstroke.

CARAVAN

Paul Henry

TRACK 13

PETITE WALTZ IN E

Paul Henry

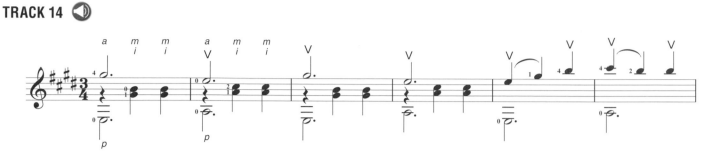

MAKING YOUR PLAYING INTERESTING

GRACE NOTES

Grace notes are the most common musical ornaments in classical guitar. They are one or more notes added to the principle note and will appear as a smaller note or notes preceding the main note. They often are notated with a slash through the ornament and a slur symbol connecting to the main note. Grace notes are played on the beat and have no rhythmic value, so they should be played very quickly and slurred to the main note.

PRACTICE TIP

It is important to play grace notes without disturbing the rhythmic tempo. So, when playing a passage with grace notes, it is best to master the passage without the grace notes first. This will allow you to later add the grace notes with a stronger sense of the rhythmic flow.

PORTAMENTO

A *portamento*, also known as a *slide* or *glissando*, is indicated by a line connecting one note to the next. To perform a portamento, play the initial note as usual; then, when shifting to the next note, keep the string depressed as you move from the first note to the second. You should hear the sliding sound as you shift. The speed of the slide may vary depending on the effect you wish to create, however much of the full value should be given to the first note. To give a slide more of a dramatic effect, you may linger on the initial note and use a slower slide while moving to the second note, thus adding a more dramatic effect to the slide. (If the landing note of a portamento is not to be plucked, a slur connecting the notes of the slide is also included in the notation; in the following example, both of the notes in each pair are plucked since a slur is not included.)

OTHER VARIATIONS

You might come across the following grace-note variations in your studies.

Grace Note Slide
When a grace note is connected to the main note with a slide, treat it rhythmically as a normal grace note. Start on the grace note and then slide quickly to the main note, but do not pluck the main note. (Notice the slur.)

Slide with Grace Note
When a slide ends with a grace note that is the same note as the arrival note, the arrival note should not be plucked, allowing the note to sound simply by arriving on the main note.

ARTICULATIONS

Exactly how each note is played in a piece is largely up to discretion of the performer's sense of style, yet there are times when a composer wants you to articulate a single note or a group of notes in a specific way. These articulations will often give a distinct feel or character to a phrase. A few of the most-used articulations and their symbols are shown in the following table.

Staccato - short, disconnected

Legato - very connected

Accent

COLOR

The *color* or *timbre* of notes that you play can be greatly affected by where you pluck the string. Playing *ponticello* means to play close to the bridge where the strings are stiffer to create a brighter, more metallic sound. This type of sound can be even sharper sounding if played using a more straight-on nail technique. Often, ponticello is used to create a distant sound or to imitate the tone of a brass instrument. Conversely, a *dolce* or sweet tone can be achieved by playing directly over or to the left of the sound hole. Experiment to find the variances on your guitar. Many guitarists will use these colors to imitate the different sounds in an orchestra. Use these colorations creatively but in appropriately stylistic ways.

PIZZICATO

Pizzicato is a technique that imitates the sound of a plucked bowed instrument such as a cello or violin. This is accomplished by resting the side of your palm on the saddle. As you reach to play the string with your thumb, your palm will tilt toward the strings, touching the strings slightly past where the strings rest on the saddle. This will slightly mute the string as you play. The more you move your palm to the left to touch more of the strings, the more the string will be muted.

Mauro Giuliani (1781–1829)

Born in Barletta, Italy, Mauro Giuliani was a cellist, singer, composer, teacher, and concert guitarist. At the age of 19, he concertized throughout Europe, earning a reputation as a guitar virtuoso. His performances helped to elevate the guitar from an accompaniment role for vocalists and violinists to a respected solo instrument. He settled in Vienna in 1806 to be part of a more sophisticated environment. His contribution to the classical guitarist's repertoire is prodigious. He produced concertos, virtuoso concert masterpieces, etudes, and pedagogic works. His compositional style reflected the Viennese style of the day: florid melodies and energetic textures showcasing the skills of the performer.

RONDO

Mauro Giuliani

TRACK 15

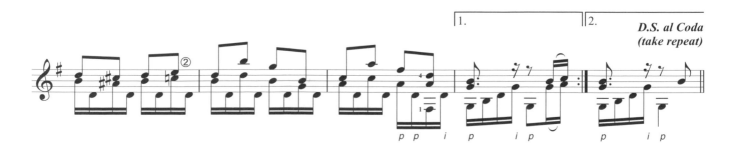

⊕ Coda

SLUR EXERCISES

These two basic slur exercises practiced daily will help greatly to bring clarity to your playing. Practice the patterns below on all six strings using the same frets as the examples. Use efficient motion when moving fingers, and keep an eye on the non-playing fingers so they stay relaxed.

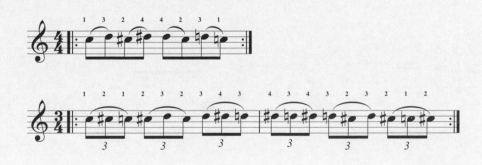

ALLEGRETTO IN E

Fernando Sor

NATURAL HARMONICS

Natural harmonics are chime-like tones played by lightly touching the string directly above certain frets (the actual fretwires, not the space between) while plucking the string normally with the right-hand fingers. They are most effectively produced on the 12th fret but also are frequently played on the 7th, 5th, and 19th frets. They can be played on every string at these frets. Most often they are used as a special effect to highlight certain notes at the beginning or end of a phrase.

NATURAL HARMONICS NOTATION

The notation for harmonics usually includes a diamond-shaped notehead. A number or Roman numeral indicating the fret position and a string indication might also be present.

NOTES PRODUCED BY PLAYING HARMONICS

Playing the harmonic at the 12th fret will produce a tone one octave higher than the open string. The harmonic at the 7th and 19th fret will produce a sound an octave-and-a-fifth higher than the open string. The harmonic at the 5th fret will produce a sound two octaves higher than the open string.

The exact notes on the 12th, 7th (and 19th), and 5th fret of each string are shown in the following example.

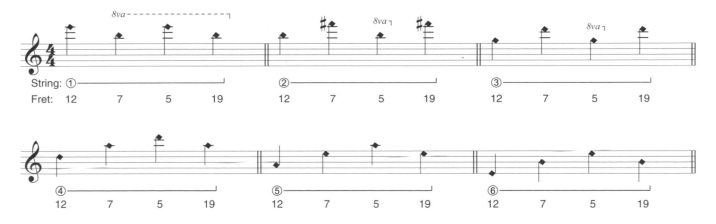

- It is important to use a light touch so as not to actually depress the string.

- Do not use the left-hand fingertips as usual; instead, use the flat part of the finger, as shown.

- Make sure to touch the string directly above the fretwire rather than between the frets.

- Immediately after the string is played, quickly remove your left-hand finger from the string to allow it to vibrate freely.

RIGHT HAND-ONLY HARMONICS TECHNIQUE

There are times when it is convenient or necessary to play harmonics with the right hand only. This will allow your left hand to continue to hold down notes if needed.

To do this, use the *i* finger of the right hand to gently touch the string above the fretwire, as before. Then, use the *a* finger of the right hand to pluck the strings.

The best results will be achieved by creating as much distance between the *i* and *a* fingers as comfortably possible.

PASTORAL

Matteo Carcassi

TRACK 17

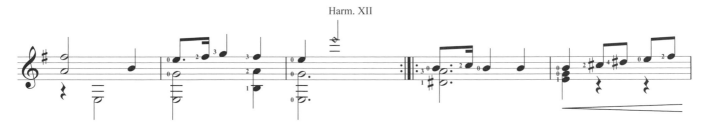

BARRES

One of the first steps to playing more complex music is the use of the *barre*. Barring is a left-hand technique that uses the first finger to press down two or more strings at the same time on the same fret. This is a major step in one's playing and will require some patience, as some degree of hand muscle development is necessary; however, once mastered, you will find a wealth of new repertoire that you will be able to play!

There are two basic types of barring: the full barre and the partial (or half) barre.

THE FULL BARRE

The *full barre* requires the player to extend the first finger fully across all six strings.

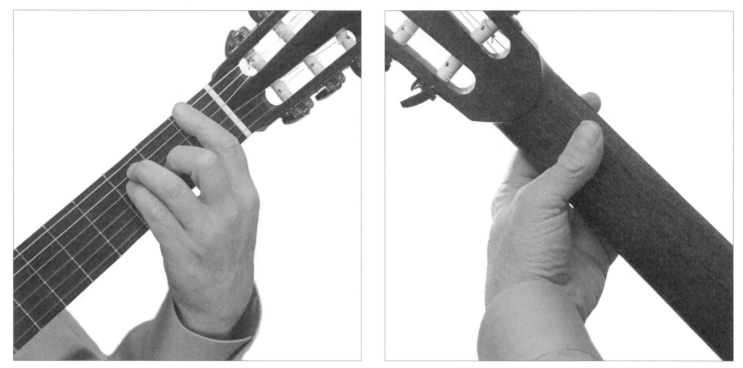

Barre Chord Front View   **Barre Chord Back View**

Rather than jumping right into some music, it is best to begin by getting comfortable with switching back and forth between two common, basic chord shapes found in every style of guitar music: the standard C major chord shape and the F major barre-chord shape.

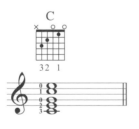

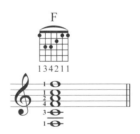

First, notice that a common finger in both chords is the 3rd finger playing the C note on the 3rd fret of the 5th string. Start by placing your fingers in the C chord shape, making sure your left thumb is placed correctly behind the neck. **The thumb placement should be the same for both chords.** When changing from the C chord to the F chord, the thumb will not need any adjustment. Without picking up your third finger, move to the F chord shape—but don't worry about pressing down yet. The first finger should be slightly tilted to the left as you barre the six strings. If you are still relaxed, your first finger should not be overly straightened; this should feel fairly comfortable. Your other three fingers should be standing on their tips without any joints collapsing. When you finally press down with all the fingers, it is most important not to change the form or shape of your fingers. Practice moving from the C chord to the F chord while keeping the thumb and third finger in place. This repeated motion will help you feel the process of integrating barring into your playing.

The following short exercise will help you to build strength and make smooth transitions as you begin integrating the use of the barre. When using a barre, make sure that any unused fingers remain in a relaxed state.

The fret to be barred is often indicated by Roman numerals. Depending on the publisher or country of origin, the instruction to barre might include the capital letter B (for barre) or the letter C (for the Spanish term *cejilla*). The fraction tells you how much of the fretboard the barre should cover.

Study No. 7 – Barre Exercise

TRACK 18

THE HALF BARRE

At times, it is necessary to barre some but not all of the strings. As in the full barre, when playing the *half barre*, the first finger should not be fully straight. As shown in the following photo, the first finger is bent at the knuckle. This is necessary in order to keep the other fingers from being positioned too far away from the fretboard.

Half Barre Notation
Half barres are often indicated simply with the additional direction "1/2" or by a slash through the letter C or B.

The following arpeggiated chord progression is based on the ever-popular "Canon in D" by Johann Pachelbel. It is an excellent exercise to gain experience getting in and out of barring situations. Once again, it is best to play this short excerpt from memory so you can watch the efficiency of your left-hand movement.

Study No. 8 – Pachelbel "Canon in D" Progression

TRACK 19

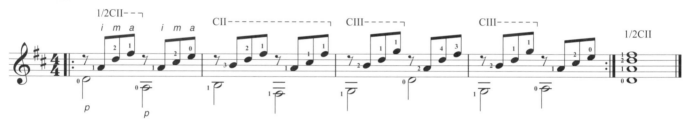

THE HINGE BARRE

The *hinge barre* is executed by simply lifting up one side of the full barre. It can be done with the tip of your finger to allow an open treble string to be played while still barring the lower strings, or you may lift just the lower portion of your finger to allow an open bass string to be played while still barring the higher strings. It is a nifty technique which can help alleviate the need to jump fingers across strings.

Treble Hinge Barre

Bass Hinge Barre

The following pieces will give you an opportunity to put different types of barres to use. Try to incorporate everything you've learned so far while working on them.

LARGHETTO

Fernando Sor

TRACK 20

REST STROKES AND WHEN TO USE THEM

In some pieces, the composer might indicate to the player where to use rest strokes; however, most of the time it is a decision that the player will make. (See Book One for review of the rest-stroke technique.) These decisions will help shape your interpretation of the piece. Rest strokes with either the thumb or finger are commonly used to highlight or give extra weight to a melodic line or accented note in the music. Being comfortable with switching in and out of rest strokes and free strokes can be a valuable tool allowing you to add extra texture to your playing. Historically, rest strokes were not typically used until the time of Tárrega (1850 to 1909); however, when playing music from an earlier period, using them in a stylistic fashion is certainly acceptable. In the following piece by Tárrega, the "V" symbol suggests the use of rest strokes on certain notes to bring out the melody.

ESTUDIO IN E MINOR

Francisco Tárrega

TRACK 21

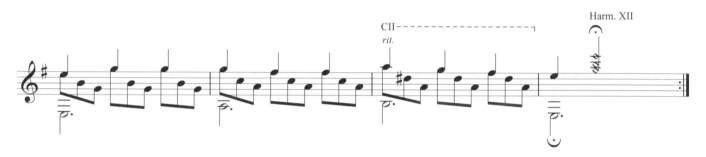

ESTUDIO IN C

Francisco Tárrega

TRACK 22

ETUDES AND STUDIES

Etudes and *studies* (or *estudios*, in Spanish) are pieces that often highlight one or two specific technical and/or musical concepts that might present a challenge to a musician. Some of these pieces are beautiful concert-worthy compositions. Composers such as Sor, Giuliani, Carcassi, Carruli, Tárrega, Villa-Lobos, and many others have contributed numerous etudes to the classical guitarist's repertoire, providing an excellent selection of music to challenge and build their skills.

Here's a short but attractive study for slurs by Tárrega.

ETUDE

Francisco Tárrega

TRACK 23

SCOTTISH FAREWELL

Traditional

TRACK 24

Wistfully

ESTUDIO

Fernando Sor

TRACK 25

Moderato

ESTUDIO

Fernando Sor

TRACK 26

Moderato

poco rit.

A Tempo

TARLETON'S RESURRECTION

John Dowland

TRACK 27

GYMNOPEDIE #1

Erik Satie

TRACK 28

Lento

*Bass hinge barre

SPANISH ROMANCE

Traditional

TRACK 29

ORNAMENTS

Ornaments are just what they sound like. They are added notes used to embellish the original notes in a musical score. They can be improvised or notated by a symbol in the music score. Every style or period of music has its own unique approach to how these ornaments are performed, so being an expert of this topic would require a significant amount of research; however, understanding a few common ornaments and performance guidelines will allow you to feel confident in your playing while you add the sparkle that ornaments provide.

Ornaments are most often performed using the left-hand slur technique on one string, but they may also be played on adjacent strings. Of course, when ornaments involve adjacent strings, most of the activity will switch to the right-hand fingers.

TRILLS

Depending on the style of music or the composer, *trills* can begin on either the upper note or the lower note. They will always finish on the main note.

MORDENTS

The *upper mordent* is executed by rapidly playing the main note followed by the higher note, then finishing on the main note.

The *lower mordent* is executed by rapidly playing the main note followed by the lower note, then finishing on the main note.

Keeping your left-hand position in mind, fingerings by the mordent will help to locate the alternate note to use. (These numbers are not always included.) For both mordents, a left-hand slurring technique is often used; however, mordents can also be played across strings with the right hand.

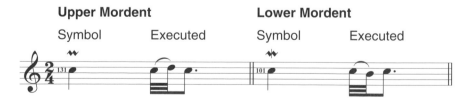

ESPAÑOLETA

Gaspar Sanz

TRACK 30

A Lute Player (Luthier)

An Example of European Lute Tablature from the Early 1600s

The following short pieces were composed by an unknown Renaissance composer for the *lute*, a popular pear-shaped instrument like the guitar. Lute composers used *tablature*, a system of writing music that uses lines depicting the strings and numbers showing the frets to be played. Lute tablature is similar to the style of tablature that some guitarists use today to write their music.

PRELUDIO

Anonymous

TRACK 31 🔊

⑥ = D

Lento

BIANCO FIORE

Anonymous

TRACK 32 🔊

⑥ = D

SCALES

Practicing scales is important to the development of many aspects of guitar playing—for both musical and technical reasons. Playing them with different rhythms, articulations, and right-hand fingerings will give you a noticeable boost in the command of your performance. While advanced players should endeavor to learn all the major and minor scales, a good start is to commit to memory a few basic movable scale patterns. Scales should be mastered using right-hand finger combinations of *i* and *m*, and *m* and *a*. Use both free stroke and rest stroke.

TRACK 33

C Major Scale - Two Octaves

C Major Scale - Two Octaves with Shift

C Melodic Minor - Two Octaves with Shift

C Harmonic Minor - Two Octaves with Shift

An important skill to develop is playing note groupings in a steady rhythm. Start by simply tapping your foot to keep a beat while playing the notes of the scale in groups of two consistently up and down the scale. Slightly accenting the first note of each group will help you keep the beat. You can then proceed to groups of three and then groups of four, both of which are more challenging.

USING A METRONOME

Using a metronome will help to ensure that you are keeping a steady rhythm. Speed is not important at first. Make sure you can play the scales repeatedly and with accuracy before increasing speed.

The following scales will help you to see note groupings of two, three, and four as you practice.

Study No. 9 – Metronome Scales 1

TRACK 34

Groupings of 2 - Eighth Notes in 2/4

Groupings of 3 - Eighth Notes in 3/8

Groupings of 4 - Sixteenth Notes in 1/4

Once keeping a steady rhythmic beat is mastered, you may use other rhythmic patterns to further refine your playing.

Study No. 10 — Metronome Scales 2

PRACTICE TIP

Playing with a metronome might not be easy at first as metronomes are perfectly accurate and unforgiving in keeping a steady beat. You might have to start with just part of the scale, playing eighth notes (groups of two) first, before you can successfully play through an entire scale.

Scale Tips

- It is very common for accomplished instrumentalists to devote a portion of their daily practice routine to playing scales.

- Using a short scale of one octave—or even just part of a scale—is an effective way to work on your speed.

- Practice scales by alternating between *i* and *m*, *m* and *a*, and also *a* and *i*. Use free strokes and rest strokes.

- Incorporate scale passages into your practice routine. Pick scales that appear in the pieces you play.

VIBRATO

Vibrato is a technique that rapidly raises and lowers the pitch of a note slightly in a pulsing fashion. It will add expression, emotion, and a lyrical quality to your playing. Vibrato in classical guitar is accomplished by gently tugging the string back and forth with your left-hand finger in a motion parallel (not perpendicular!) to the string. The speed of the vibrato may be varied to produce different effects. A slow vibrato will create a more lyrical or romantic quality, while speeding up the pulse will have a more intense effect.

The finger should remain firmly pressed to the string. Use the relaxed motion of your forearm and wrist to push and pull the string. Most guitarists find it easier at first to use vibrato with their 2nd or 3rd finger as it is easier to achieve a relaxed and even motion with the middle fingers. With practice, each finger will begin to feel comfortable with the technique. Practicing vibrato by using a two-octave major scale without a shift in the middle of fretboard is a good way to get a feel for vibrato. This is because the strings will feel less stiff in the middle of the neck. Practice slowly and with a relaxed feel to get consistent vibrato on each note.

The following composition by Matteo Carcassi is from his well-known collection *25 Melodic and Progressive Studies, Op. 60*. It is an excellent piece to test your skill with scales and dynamics.

STUDY #1 OP. 60

Matteo Carcassi

TRACK 35

PLAYING SOLO MELODIES

When playing solo melody lines, guitarists will try to avoid open strings and often choose instead to finger the notes on middle or upper frets. This will allow for more effective use of vibrato and give more color and vibrancy to your tone.

The following duet, a medley of two famous old English melodies, will give the guitarist playing the top part a great opportunity to create lyrical lines with effective use of vibrato and a legato tone, using rest strokes throughout. The second guitar part is a challenging non-stop arpeggio accompaniment.

Note: When two notes of the same pitch are placed right next to each other with different time values and stems, it indicates that a single note is functioning in both the higher and lower voice of the music. Only one single note should be played.

GREENSLEEVES/SCARBOROUGH FAIR

Traditional

TRACK 36 🔊

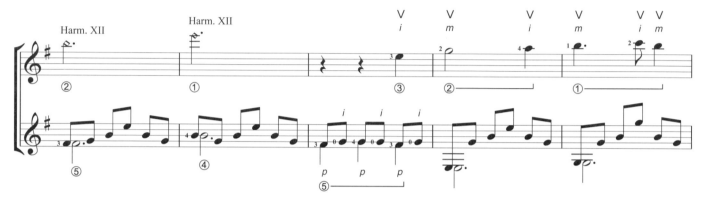

Harm. XII

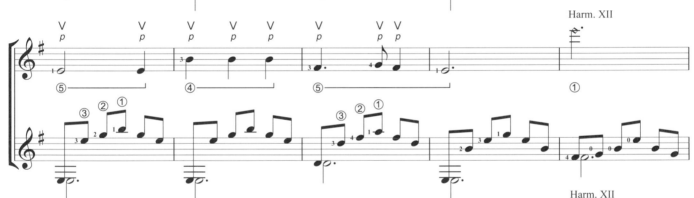

Harm. XII

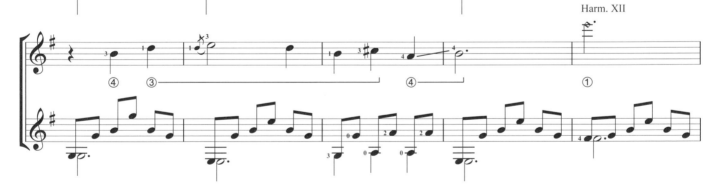

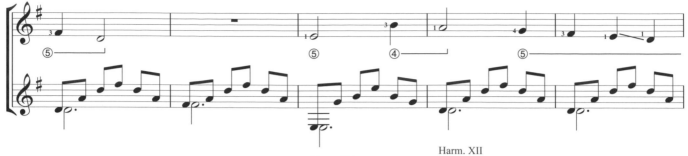

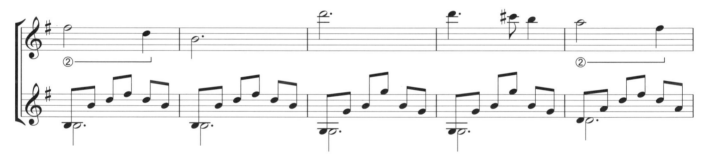

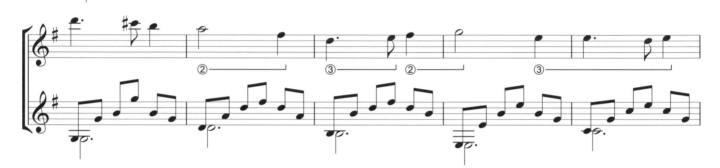

ARTIFICIAL HARMONICS

While natural harmonics are all played on open strings, *artificial harmonics* are produced by fretting a note and then using the right hand-only technique to touch the string twelve frets higher than the fretted note. When doing this, you will be touching the string exactly halfway between the fretted note and the bridge.

The actual harmonic note being played will always be an octave above the fretted note. This technique allows you a full palette of notes using harmonics, making it possible to play melodic passages using harmonics. Your thumb is also available to play bass notes along with the melody, as in the last line of the following selection "Black Is the Color of My True Love's Hair."

In the photo above, the left-hand plays an F# on the 2nd fret while the right hand uses the right hand-only technique to touch and pluck the same string twelve frets higher on the 14th fret. This produces an F# harmonic.

ARTIFICIAL HARMONICS NOTATION

Notation of artificial harmonics will often include an octave symbol, meaning the actual pitch will sound one octave above what is written. Also included are the fret number and circled string number showing where the note will be plucked.

"Black Is the Color of My True Love's Hair" is based on a song from Scotland which found its way into the Appalachian culture. It has a haunting melody that travels from the higher notes to the bass notes, also moving into artificial harmonics. Try to keep the melody in the forefront as you change between registers.

BLACK IS THE COLOR OF MY TRUE LOVE'S HAIR

Anonymous

TRACK 37

COUNTERPOINT

When two or more melodies are played simultaneously it is called *counterpoint*. Playing two melodies at once can be a technical challenge. Care must be taken to make sure that every note in both voices is held for its full time value. It can become a musical challenge to make sure that each melody is played with the usual attention to articulation and dynamics. Take time to play each melody separately, or better yet, find another player to play the two voices together in duet fashion. This will give you a better sense of the phrasing before combining the parts. The Baroque period (1600–1750) was a time when contrapuntal music flourished with composers such as Vivaldi, Purcell, Handel, Scarlatti, Telemann, Monteverdi and, of course, the great master J.S. Bach.

ARIA

G.A. Brescianello

TRACK 38

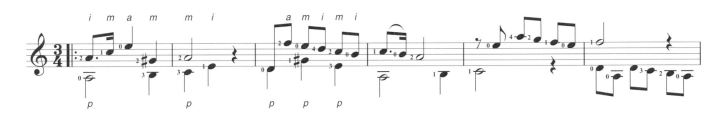

MENUETT

Johann Krieger

AIR

Henry Purcell

GAVOTTE

G.A. Brescianello

TRACK 41

HORNPIPE

Henry Purcell

TRACK 42

KEEPING AN EYE ON YOUR TECHNIQUE

RIGHT-HAND TECHNIQUE

As you perform more-complex pieces, it is always a good idea to check on how you are doing with basic right-hand concepts. Often, if greater attention is given to the left-hand work, certain right-hand fundamentals might need a review.

Sitting Position

The relaxation of your right hand is directly related to your sitting position. Make sure your right arm is positioned on top of the guitar, allowing your right hand to be naturally positioned in front of the strings with a relaxed wrist.

Finger Motion

Check to make sure that each finger is able to play with an independent, concise motion without triggering any unwanted movement or tension in any of the other fingers. Also, make sure that each finger uses the same approach to playing the strings (as described in Book One). Aim for pleasant, consistent tone production.

The Thumb

When playing the strings with your fingers, it is important to be sure that the thumb stays in a relaxed state. Do not allow your finger movements to create tension in the thumb.

Fingering

Use logical fingering, alternating fingers for scale passages and otherwise fully incorporating all three fingers (*i*, *m*, and *a*) in a logical way.

LEFT-HAND TECHNIQUE

Relaxing the Non-Playing Fingers

As you play, you might find that certain fingers not being used will involuntarily move away, recoil, or open up away from their relaxed position. The fingers should simply hover directly over the strings. To check this, slowly play a memorized scale. Watch your fingers carefully—not the finger that is playing the note, but rather the other three fingers. (Using a mirror is often a helpful tool.) Check for any extra unwanted finger motion. The fourth finger is often the worst offender; however, you might have the same issue with the other fingers. This unwanted movement is most often caused by unnecessary tension. The key to fix this is to play as slowly as needed to intercept the unnecessary movement before it occurs. Once the involuntary movement is controlled, you will be able to gradually increase speed while minimizing unnecessary movement.

Thumb Placement

Be sure to check that your thumb is in the proper position as that will greatly affect the efficient movement of your left-hand fingers. If the left thumb is not behind the neck properly but instead sits too far toward the top part of the neck, your left-hand fingers will most likely open up as you release a string, causing excess finger motion.

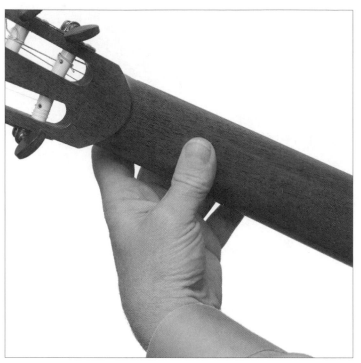

Proper Thumb Placement

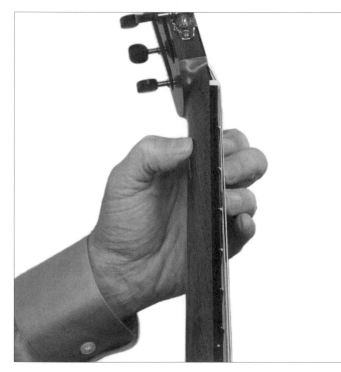
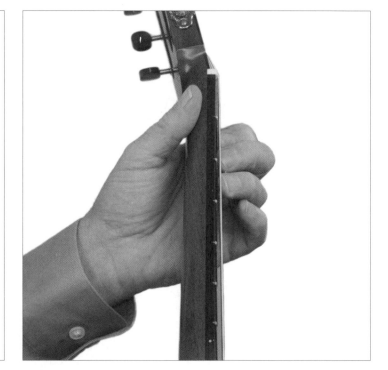

Improper Thumb Placement

FRANCISCO TÁRREGA (1852–1909)

Francisco Tárrega was born in 1852 in Villareal, Spain. His father insisted that he study piano as well as the guitar, as the guitar at that time was not considered to be a respected instrument. He entered the Madrid Conservatory in 1877 and studied piano and music theory. He later earned his living as a teacher and concert performer, giving concerts on both piano and guitar. He composed an impressive collection of important compositions and arranged numerous works of major composers including Bach, Beethoven, Schubert, Granados, Handel, and Chopin. His innovative approach to right-hand technique and his composing style—which used the full spectrum of the guitar's pallet of sounds—helped the guitar to become popular on the concert stage.

LAGRIMA

Francisco Tárrega

TRACK 43 🔊

PAVANA

Francisco Tárrega

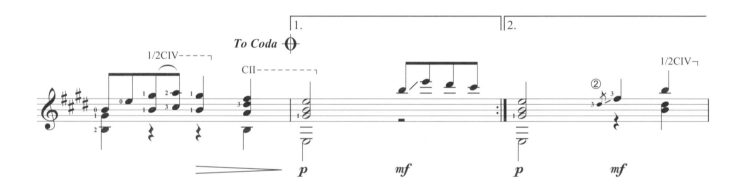

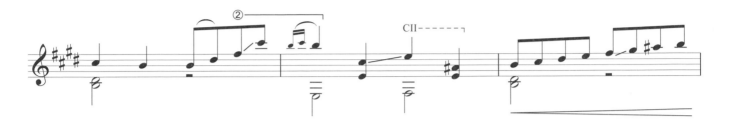

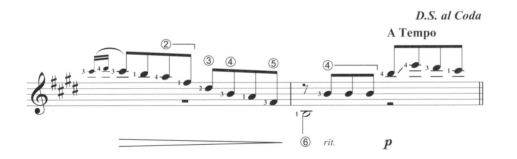

ADELITA

Francisco Tárrega

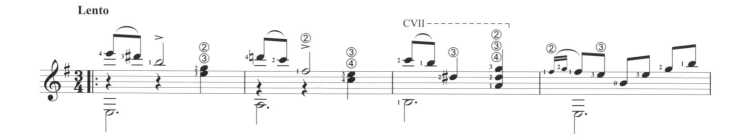

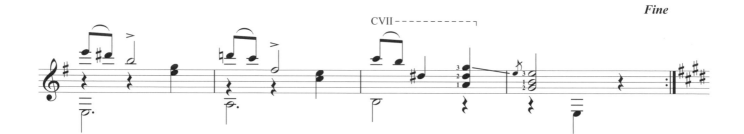

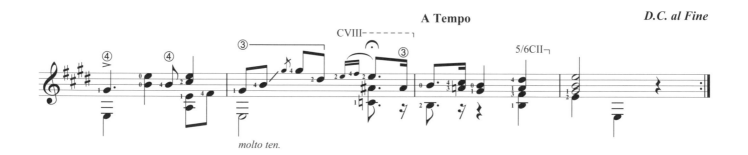

J.S. BACH (1685–1750)

Bach never composed for the guitar; however, arrangements of his music have become centerpieces in the classical guitarist's repertoire. His compositions for both solo violin and violin-cello may easily be performed with little or no alteration. Bach often adapted his compositions so they could be played on different instruments than originally intended.

MUSETTE

J.S. Bach

TRACK 46

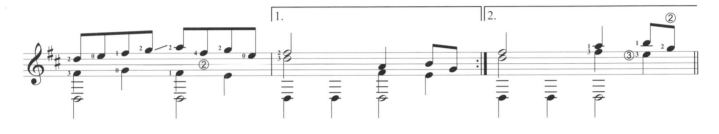

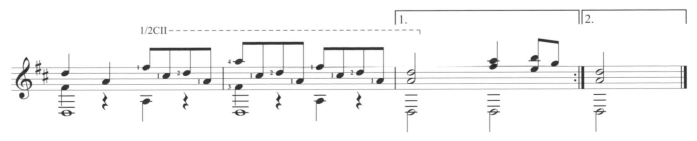

BOURRÉE IN E MINOR

J.S. Bach

TRACK 47

PRELUDE FROM CELLO SUITE NO. 1

J.S. Bach

TRACK 48

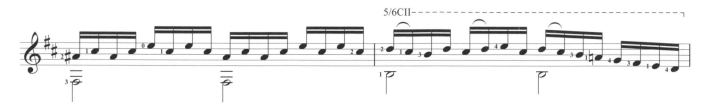

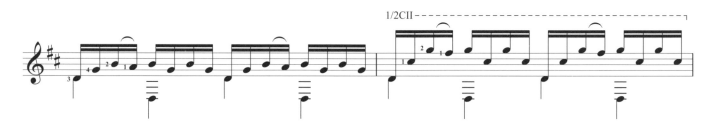

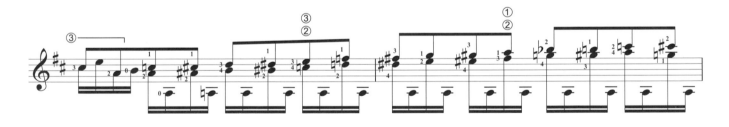

NICCOLÒ PAGANINI (1782–1840)

SONATINA

Niccolò Paganini

TRACK 49

Allegro

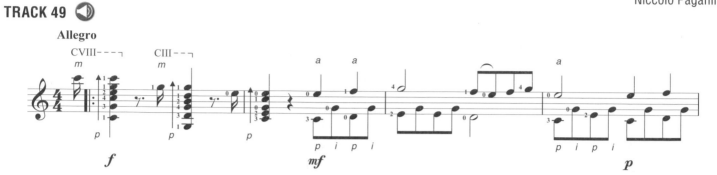

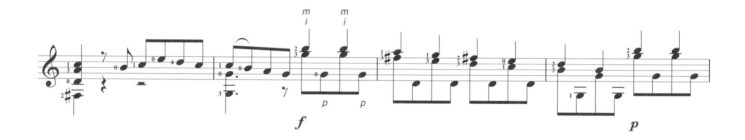

68

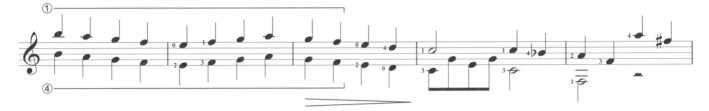

MATTEO CARCASSI (1792–1853)
STUDY #7 OP. 60

Matteo Carcassi

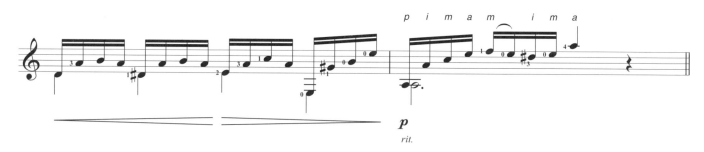

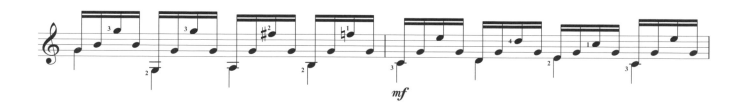

STUDY #10 OP. 60

Matteo Carcassi

GASPAR SANZ (1640–1710)

Born in 1640 to a wealthy family in the Aragon region in northeastern Spain, Sanz was a composer, organist, priest, and guitarist. He studied the Italian style of guitar in Rome and later returned to Spain, writing the first major method book for guitar (published in 1674). He composed many short works for guitar written in the style of the melodies and dances in fashion at the time. His most famous piece, "Canarios," is still a crowd favorite today with its shifting meter and catchy dance rhythms.

PAVANAS

Gaspar Sanz

TRACK 52

CANARIOS

Gaspar Sanz

TRACK 53

IN THE SPANISH STYLE: FLAMENCO

Flamenco is a music and dance style which has its roots of the Andalusia region in southern Spain. It features passionate melodies and infectious dance rhythms. These alluring qualities have had a strong influence on classical guitar. The following flamenco-style dance piece will require the use of a few colorful techniques that are common in flamenco music and now regularly found in the classical guitarist's repertoire.

Golpe

Golpe simply means to hit the guitar with the right hand. The type of sound you wish to create or the amount of time you have to execute the golpe will play a part in how you choose to hit the guitar. Often, it will be a tap with a finger on the soundboard below the strings or near the bridge. Another common option is to slap the fingerboard and strings near the upper frets with an open right hand. This latter approach also functions to stop the strings from ringing and will help to punctuate the rhythm.

Tremolo

Tremolo is an arpeggiated right-hand technique in which the thumb plays a note on the lower strings, and fingers *a*, *m*, and *i* play repeated notes on a higher string. This technique may feature a melody either on the higher notes or the lower notes.

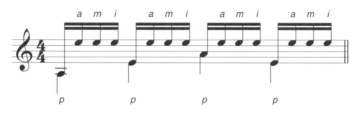

Rasgueado

Rasgueado is a form of strumming used in flamenco music which can use the thumb and all four fingers. The little finger (usually labeled *c* or *e*) is sometimes included to help execute some very exciting rhythms. There are a myriad of possible combinations of finger patterns and rhythms, ranging from simple upward and downward strokes with one finger to more complex patterns using all the fingers. The direction of each strum is shown with arrows.

Upward arrow: strum downward from the bass strings to the treble strings.

Downward arrow: strum upward from the treble strings to the bass strings.

Training each finger to independently play downward or upward strokes in a precise rhythm will most likely require some degree of slow, patient practice. It is important to let the fingers move only from the big knuckle without wrist or hand movement. Initially, placing your thumb on the low E string might help stabilize your hand. To start, look at the following two basic patterns. Example 2 uses all four fingers: *p*, *i*, *m*, and *e*. Remember, you should strive to play the precise rhythm, not just the finger-strumming pattern in general.

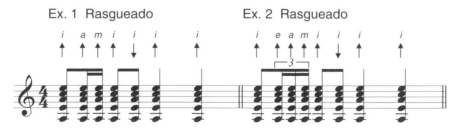

The *farruca* is one of many dances in the flamenco style. Keeping a steady beat is imperative as you navigate through the variety of rhythms. Note the final rasgueado ends with a downward thumb stroke to complete the *e-a-m-i-p* pattern.

FARRUCA

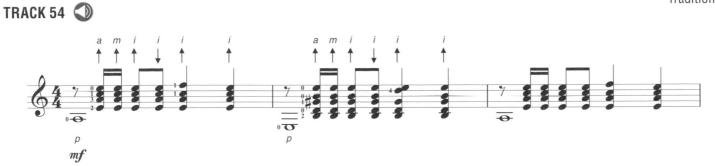

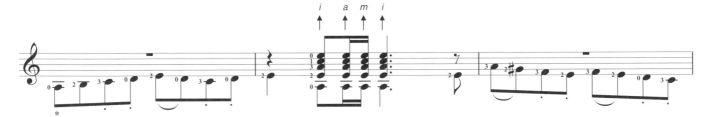

*When not part of a chord, pick all downstemmed notes throughout with *p*.

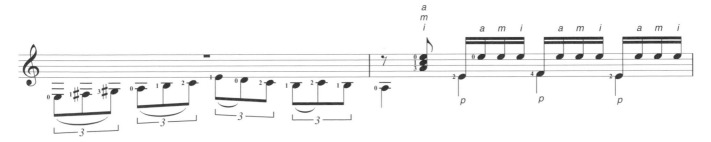

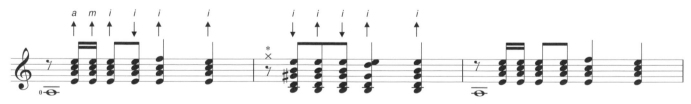

*Golpe: Strike the strings and fretboard on the
upper frets. Follow through with an index-finger
stroke to play the following eighth-note chord.

Final words: There is a tremendous amount of music, new and old, that will certainly challenge you and further spark your interest… Explore.

"The guitar is the easiest instrument to play and the hardest to play well."

—Andrés Segovia

HAL LEONARD
CLASSICAL GUITAR METHOD

A Beginner's Guide with Step-by-Step Instruction and Over 25 Pieces to Study and Play
BY PAUL HENRY

The *Hal Leonard Classical Guitar Method* is designed for anyone just learning to play classical guitar. This comprehensive and easy-to-use beginner's guide by renowned classical guitarist and teacher Paul Henry uses the music of the master composers to teach you the basics of the classical style and technique. The accompanying audio features all the pieces in the book for demonstration and play along. Includes pieces by Beethoven, Bach, Mozart, Schumann, Giuliani, Carcassi, Bathioli, Aguado, Tarrega, Purcell, and more. Includes all the basics plus info on PIMA technique, two- and three-part music, time signatures, key signatures, articulation, free stroke, rest stroke, composers, and much more. Does NOT include tablature. Audio is accessed online using the unique code inside each book and can be downloaded or streamed. The audio also includes **PLAYBACK+** features such as tempo adjustment, looping, and other features to assist with practice.

00697376 Book/Online Audio..$16.99

HAL LEONARD CLASSICAL GUITAR METHOD – TAB EDITION
BY PAUL HENRY
00142652 Book/Online Audio..$17.99

ALSO AVAILABLE

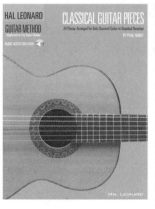

CLASSICAL GUITAR PIECES
24 Pieces Arranged for Solo Guitar in Standard Notation
BY PAUL HENRY

A great supplement to the *Hal Leonard Classical Guitar Method*, this songbook with online audio features 24 pieces ideal for students to play, including: Allegretto (Fernando Carulli) • Allegro (Wolfgang Mozart) • Andante (Matteo Carcassi) • Andante in C (Fernando Sor) • Estudio (Fernando Sor) • Orlando Sleepeth (John Dowland) • Pastorale (Matteo Carcassi) • Simple Gifts (American Traditional) • and more. Please note this book does not include tablature. The audio is accessed online using the unique code inside each book and can be streamed or downloaded. The audio files include **PLAYBACK+**, a multi-functional audio player that allows you to slow down audio without changing pitch, set loop points, change keys, and pan left or right.

00697388 Book/Online Audio..$12.99

HAL LEONARD FLAMENCO GUITAR METHOD

Learn to Play Flamenco Guitar with Step-by-Step Lessons and Authentic Pieces to Study and Play
BY HUGH BURNS

Here's your complete guide to learning flamenco guitar! This method uses traditional Spanish flamenco song forms and classical pieces to teach you the basics of this style and technique. You'll learn to play in the style of Paco de Lucia, Sabicas, Niño Ricardo and Ramón Montoya. Lessons cover: strumming, picking and percussive techniques; arpeggios; improvisation; fingernail tips; capos; and much more. Includes flamenco history and a glossary, and both standard notation and tab. The book also includes online access to 58 professionally recorded tracks for demonstration and play-along.

00697363 Book/Online Audio..$17.99

Prices, contents, and availability subject to change without notice.

HAL•LEONARD®
www.halleonard.com